Contents

*Words in **bold** are in the glossary on page 30

Game, set and match

Tennis is a fast-paced ball and racquet sport for either two individual players (singles) or two pairs of players (doubles). The ball is hit across a court divided by a net into two halves. Top **professional** tennis players are phenomenal athletes, able to sprint, leap and change direction quickly. During matches they perform to the top of their ability for hours on end.

Tennis courts

Tennis players compete against each other at competitions called tournaments. Different court surfaces, such as grass and clay, are used. These varying surfaces can affect the speed and height of the ball as it bounces and influence what sort of play and tactics a player will use.

Point scoring

Each point in a game is started with an overhead shot called a **serve**, which puts the ball into play. Players return the ball looking to force their opponent into making a mistake, called an error, or to hit a winning shot themselves.

Top women's player Serena Williams of the USA hits a powerful return during the Australian Open Championship. Tennis at the Australian Open is played on hard asphalt courts.

Winning a match

A tennis match is divided into sets. Matches are usually the best of three sets for women and five sets for men. To win a set, a player has to win six games and be two games ahead of their opponent, so a score of 6–4 wins the set, but 6–5 means that further games must be played until one player is two games clear. Players swop serve between each game.

GREAT SPORTING STATS

Tie-breakers

In most tournaments, if a set reaches six games each, the set then moves into a **tie-break.** One player serves the first point, then the serve switches between players every two points. The aim is to score seven or more points and be two points ahead of an opponent. With no tie-break allowed in the final set of some tennis tournaments, matches can last a long time. In 2010 John Isner, of the USA, beat French player Nicolas Mahut at the Wimbledon tournament. The fifth set ended 70 games to 68 and lasted over 11 hours!

Points scoring in a game:
Love – 0 points
15 – 1 point
30 – 2 points
40 – 3 points
Deuce – both players are tied at 40–40. They need to win two points in a row from that position to win the game.
Advantage – this is the point won by a player after deuce.
Game – the player has won the game and a new game starts.

An exhausted John Isner raises his arms after beating Nicolas Mahut at Wimbledon. The final match score was 6–4, 3–6, 6–7, 7–6, 70–68. The match lasted 11 hours and 5 minutes.

COURT No. 18

The ATP Tour

The Association of Tennis Professionals (**ATP**) was founded in 1972. It runs the top level of tournaments in men's tennis, comprising hundreds of events all over the world.

US player Pete Sampras was ranked ATP world number one at the end of six consecutive years (1993–1998), an all-time record.

Different levels

Tournaments are set at different levels. Futures events are the third highest level and Challenger events the second highest. Players in these events try to win enough tournaments and ranking points (see page 7) to allow them to compete in the highest level of tournaments, such as the ATP 250, 500 and 1000 events and the four Grand Slams (see pages 12–13).

One long season

The ATP tennis season is very long with tournaments, such as the Brisbane Open in Australia, starting in early January and the World Tour Finals (see pages 10–11) held near the end of November. Players need to stay fit and focused throughout the year to continue to compete at the top of their game.

Ranking points

Players' performances are ranked against each other by a points system known as the world rankings. The more matches a player wins in a tournament, the more ranking points he receives. Bigger tournaments, such as Wimbledon and the US Open, offer more points than smaller competitions. A player's points total gives him a position in the world ranking. The top-ranked players get to play in the biggest tournaments. The prize money can be huge. Swiss tennis legend Roger Federer has won over US$92 million (about £59 million) in prize money in tournaments.

Number of weeks ranked number one on the ATP Tour:

Roger Federer 302
Pete Sampras 286
Ivan Lendl 270
Jimmy Connors 268
John McEnroe 170

Twin brothers Bob and Mike Bryan, of the USA, during the doubles final of the ATP World Tour Finals, 2009. As a doubles pair, they hold the record for over ten year-end rankings at number one.

The WTA Tour

The Women's Tennis Association (**WTA**) was formed in 1973 by female tennis players who wanted to compete at the top level. It has been a spectacular success.

Wealthy WTA

Since the WTA Tour began, more than 324 players have each earned over US$1 million (£640,000) in prize money. Unlike in the past, prize money over the last ten years has matched that of similar men's tournaments in many events. This helped Belgium's Justine Henin to become the first woman in any sport to win US$5 million in prize money in a single year (2007).

Tour format

In 2015, the WTA calendar included a total of 55 tournaments in addition to four Grand Slam titles. These are divided into 21 Premier and 32 International tournaments, and two year-end championships. The tournaments were played in 32 different countries with a total prize money of more than US$129 million (£84 million). Above the Premier Tournaments in status are the four **Grand Slams**. Nearly all of the tournaments are in a **knockout** format. The players play the best of three sets and the winners progress to the next round.

Justine Henin wins a point during a US Open match against Serena Williams in 2007. Henin retired in 2011, having won 43 WTA tournaments during her career.

World rankings

Players are awarded ranking points for every win. These range from as many as 2,000 for winning a Grand Slam, to one point for being knocked out in the first round of a minor tournament. Every week during the tennis season (January to late November) the WTA publishes the world rankings. This is a list of players ranked on the number of points they have amassed. In July 2015, the USA's Serena Williams became the first number one ranked player to hold more than twice as many points as the number two player.

GREAT SPORTING STATS

Serena Williams is one of eight US players who have been ranked WTA number one. German player Steffi Graf holds the record for the most weeks at the top with an astounding 377 weeks. This equals seven and a quarter years!

Victoria Azarenka on court at the 2012 US Open. In July 2012, Azarenka became WTA number one and remained so for 32 weeks.

End of season showdowns

At the end of the tennis season, the leading eight players from both the ATP and WTA Tours take part in an end of season competition, with ranking points and big prize money at stake. The men's competition in 2014, for example, offered 900 ranking points plus US$1,455,000 (approx £927,520) to the winner.

Change of names

There has been an end of season ATP Tour finale since 1970. It was originally known as the Masters Grand Prix tournament. From 2000 to 2008, it was called the Tennis Masters Cup, and in 2009 it became known as the ATP World Tour Finals. Since 2009, it has been held at the 23,000 capacity O_2 Arena in London.

Roger Federer poses with the trophy after beating Jo-Wilfried Tsonga in the final of the 2011 ATP World Tour Finals.

Showdown in London

The eight-day men's competition begins with the eight players divided into groups of four, who play each other. This is called a 'round robin' format. The two leading players from each group contest semi-finals to determine the finalists. The same format is used to determine the winners from the eight leading men's doubles pairs. In 2014, the US twins Bob and Mike Bryan, also victorious in 2003, 2004 and 2009, won the event.

WTA Finals

The women's end of season event began in 1972 and has been held in various cities around the world. In 2014, after stints in Doha, Qatar and Istanbul, Turkey, the tournament moved to Singapore. It is played over six days at the Singapore Indoor Stadium, where a crowd of 10,000 can watch the sporting action.

Sister act

The eight leading women in singles and the top four doubles pairs take part in the event, which has the same format as the ATP World Tour Finals. In 2008, Venus Williams won the event. The following year she lost to her sister, Serena, in the final. Serena also won the event in 2001, 2012, 2013 and 2014, joining Steffi Graf as a five-time winner.

Russian tennis star Maria Sharapova reacts after winning a game in the WTA finals.

GREAT SPORTING STATS

In 2014, there was a total of US$6.5 million (£4.3 million) prize money on offer at the WTA Finals. The winners and runners-up received:

Singles*
Winner: US$2,190,000 (£1,440,410)
Runner-up: US$1,114,000 (£732,702)

Doubles (per pair)
Winner: $500,000 (£328,861)
Runners-up: $250,000 (£164,430)

(* Figures based on players winning all three matches in the round robin stage)

Grand Slams

Four annual tournaments hold greater prestige and appeal to players and fans than all the rest. These are the tennis majors or Grand Slam tournaments. Spaced out over the tennis season, these are the tournaments for which **elite** players try to reach their peak in order to win.

The big four

The Australian Open, French Open, Wimbledon Championships and the US Open are the four Grand Slam tournaments. Each holds competitions for **veterans** and juniors, as well as singles, doubles and **mixed doubles** competitions for the very best players in the world.

Varying challenges

The Grand Slam tournaments are played on different court surfaces. Clay is used for the French Open. This slow surface results in long, energy-sapping **rallies** from the back of the court. Wimbledon is played on grass which promotes shorter, more explosive points, with **serve and volley** tactics often used. The Australian and US Opens are played on asphalt hard courts, which are faster than clay but slower than grass.

Don Budge, of the USA, competes against England's Bunny Austin at the 1938 Wimbledon men's final. In 1938, Budge became the first man to win all four Grand Slam events in the same year.

Massive appeal

Each of the Grand Slam tournaments attracts huge crowds. The very first Wimbledon Championships, in 1877, saw about 200 spectators pay to watch. In 2015, 484,391 people came to watch the 13 days of tennis. Even more went to watch the action at the bigger **stadia** of the US Open. In 2015, over 700,000 spectators attended.

Slam superstars

Winning one Grand Slam tournament is a great achievement, but some phenomenal players have won several. In 2009, Roger Federer won his fifteenth Grand Slam singles title, beating the record set by US player Pete Sampras. In women's tennis, Australian player Margaret Court won 24 Grand Slam titles and had an incredible record at the Australian Open, winning 11 of the 12 singles finals she reached in the 1960s and 1970s.

GREAT SPORTING STATS

Most Grand Slam singles titles:

Men
1. Roger Federer (Switzerland) 17
2. Pete Sampras (USA) 14 and Rafael Nadal (Spain) 14
3. Roy Emerson (Australia) 12
4. Rod Laver (Australia) 11 and Björn Borg (Sweden) 11

Women
1. Margaret Court (Australia) 24
2. Steffi Graf (Germany) 22
3. Serena Williams (USA) 21
4. Helen Wills Moody (USA) 19

Serena Williams and Justine Henin play the final of the 2010 Australian Open in the packed Rod Laver Arena.

The Australian Open

The Australian Open (originally the Australasian Tennis Championship) was first held in 1905 at the Warehouseman's Cricket Ground in Melbourne. After over 50 years of moving around Australia, the tournament found a permanent home back in Melbourne, at Melbourne Park, where it will remain until 2036 at least.

Early start

The Australian Open is held in the middle of January. With the previous season having ended in late November, it provides an early test of players' fitness and form at the start of the new tennis season.

Extreme heat policy

Held in the middle of the hot summer, players at the Australian Open have sometimes suffered from heat exhaustion and have had to give up matches – known as defaulting. Since 1998, an extreme heat policy has operated. When daytime temperatures reach 40°C, matches can be halted, rest gaps extended and arena roofs closed to keep players cool.

Overcome by heat, Serbia's Novak Djokovic towels his brow after retiring from his 2009 Australian Open match against Andy Roddick.

Roofed arenas

Melbourne Park is currently the only Grand Slam venue to have three courts with retractable roofs. These roofs slide over to shield the courts from rain and strong sunshine. The largest of its show courts holds 14,820 people. Originally called Centre Court, it was renamed the Rod Laver Arena in 2000 after the great Australian player. Laver was the only person to win all four Grand Slam tournaments in a single year twice over, in 1962 and 1969.

Winning streak

Margaret Court holds the record for the most Australian Open wins with 11 singles wins, plus 12 further doubles and mixed doubles titles. An unusual record occurred in both 2009 and 2010, when pairs of brothers (Mike and Bob Bryan) and sisters (Serena and Venus Williams) won the doubles competitions.

Margaret Smith (later Margaret Court), of Australia, plays a shot at the 1960 Australian Open. She went on to win the tournament at the tender age of 17.

GREAT SPORTING STATS

The prize money for the 2015 tournament:

Men's and women's singles
Winners Aus$3,100,000 (£1,445,560)
Runners-up Aus$1,550,000 (£722,780)
Semi-finalists Aus$650,000 (£303,100)
Quarter-finalists Aus$340,000 (£158,545)

Doubles (per pair)
Winners Aus$575,000 (£268,130)
Runners-up Aus$285,000 (£132,900)

Mixed doubles (per pair)
Winners Aus$142,500 (£66,450)
Runners-up Aus$71,500 (£33,340)

The French Open

First held in 1891, the French Open moved to its current home of Stade Roland Garros in Paris, France, in 1928. Play begins on a Sunday in late May each year. The French Open is the premier clay court tournament and pushes players to the limit.

A large crowd watches Serena Williams play Japan's Ai Sugiyama during the fourth round of the French Open.

Roland Garros

Named after a famous French aviator, Roland Garros is home to 20 tennis courts, the largest being Court Philippe Chatrier, which holds 14,840 spectators. Plans are now underway for a major extension to Roland Garros, including the fitting of a retractable roof over Court Philippe Chatrier.

Clay court tennis

Roland Garros's slow clay courts mean players have long rallies, often from the back of the court. Patience and incredible fitness are required in order to win matches. In 2004, two male French singles players, Fabrice Santoro and Arnaud Clément, battled their match out for a lung-busting 6 hours 33 minutes, with Santoro winning the final set 16-14.

Player numbers

The men's and women's singles competitions feature 128 players who must play and win six matches to reach the final. The men's title was won in 2015 by the Swiss player Stanislas Wawrinka and the women's by Serena Williams. The doubles competitions feature 64 male and 64 female doubles pairs, whilst the mixed doubles see 32 pairs battle it out. Prize money is equal for men and women, with the winners of the singles each receiving €800,000 (£1,306,090).

Record breakers

Some players are better suited to clay courts and flourish at the French Open, such as Justine Henin, who won four women's singles titles there in five years (2003, 2005–2007), and US player Chris Evert, who won seven women's singles there in total. The youngest winners are the US player Michael Chang in 1989, aged 17, and Monica Seles, from the former Yugoslavia, in 1990, aged 16.

GREAT SPORTING STATS

Spanish player Rafael Nadal set an amazing French Open record in 2015. His victory over US player Jack Sock was his 39th win in a row at the tournament. Prior to that, his record had been 31 consecutive wins. However, Serbian Novak Djokovic prevented the nine-time French Open champion Nadal from winning his 40th consecutive match, with a defeat of 7–5, 6–3, 6–1.

Spain's Rafael Nadal has been virtually unbeatable at Roland Garros, losing just two matches in 12 years and winning the French Open nine times in ten years (2005–2014).

Wimbledon

First held in 1877, the Wimbledon Championships was the first of the Grand Slam tournaments, and is the oldest professional tennis tournament. It is run by the All England Lawn Tennis Club in southwest London and is held every year over two weeks, beginning in the last week of June.

Novak Djokovic in action against Roger Federer in the 2015 Wimbledon men's singles final. Djokovic won the match in four sets.

Played on grass

Wimbledon is the only Grand Slam tournament held on grass courts, and play begins shortly after the **clay court season**. Most entrants try to play warm-up tournaments on grass in Germany or Britain in the weeks before the tournament to get used to grass's fast pace and occasionally unpredictable bounce. They need to adapt their game accordingly.

Centre court

The tournament is played on 19 courts – three main show courts and 16 outside courts. Number One Court holds about 11,000 people while the tournament's ultimate venue, Centre Court, holds about 15,000. Many thousands of fans mill around Aorangi Park, next to Centre Court, watching matches on giant screens.

Retractable roof

In 2009, Centre Court's new retractable roof, built in response to frequent rain delays at the tournament, was used for the first time. The first full game with the roof closed was a fourth round men's singles match in 2009 between Britain's Andy Murray and Stanislas Wawrinka from Switzerland.

Wild cards

Several weeks before the tournament begins, Wimbledon's organisers invite players to take part whose rankings aren't high enough for them to qualify automatically. These invitations are called wild cards. They are given to players who have performed well in previous tournaments and are trying to make a comeback, or to players who stimulate public interest. In 2001, Croatian Goran Ivanišević was ranked 125th in the world, but he received a wild card for Wimbledon. He went on to win the men's singles, a feat no wild card entrant had ever achieved before.

GREAT SPORTING STATS

Czech American Martina Navratilova's record at Wimbledon is nothing short of extraordinary. Her first match there was in 1973 and her last an incredible 33 years later. She played 326 matches at Wimbledon, the most of any player.

Singles
Won 120 matches and 9 championships

Doubles
Won 100 matches and 7 championships

Mixed doubles
Won 56 matches and 4 championships

Martina Navratilova wipes away a tear as she holds the Wimbledon ladies' singles trophy. This win in 1990 was Navratilova's ninth Wimbledon singles title.

The US Open

The US Open is one of the oldest major tennis tournaments, first contested in 1881. It is held over two weeks in late August and September, and is known for its noisy, excitable crowds. Up to 24,000 people cram into its main stadium, named after the 1968 men's singles winner, Arthur Ashe.

Different surfaces

Up until 1974, the US Open was played on grass, but complaints about variable bounce saw the tournament trial clay courts for three years (1975–77). In 1978, the tournament moved to Flushing Meadows–Corona Park in New York City where the court surfaces are made of hard asphalt. American Jimmy Connors is the only player to have won US Open titles on all three surfaces.

Feeling blue

In 2005, all of the tournament's courts were coloured blue with the surrounding area green. This was designed to make the ball more visible to the players and spectators. From 2016, a retractable roof will also be a feature to avoid rain delays and the effects of strong winds.

Jimmy Connors reaches for the ball during the 1992 US Open tournament. Connors won the US Open men's singles five times.

Great winners

American players Jimmy Connors and Pete Sampras have both won the US Open men's singles five times, and Chris Evert triumphed in the women's singles six times. Martina Navratilova managed only four women's singles, but added nine doubles and three mixed doubles titles to her haul. She won her last US Open mixed doubles title with Bob Bryan in 2006 at the age of 49.

Amazing comebacks

The 2009 US Open saw an amazing performance from Belgian Kim Clijsters who had just come out of retirement after having her first child. She wasn't **seeded**, but went on to beat Dane Caroline Wozniacki in the final. She won again in 2010. A similarly epic performance occurred in the men's singles, where Argentinian Juan Martin del Potro defeated the top two players in the world (Rafael Nadal and Roger Federer) to secure the trophy. Nadal bounced back to win the title in 2010 and 2013.

GREAT SPORTING STATS

Players taking part in the 2015 US Open competed for a prize pot totalling more than US$42 million (£27.5 million). The winner of the men's and women's singles final took away US$3.3 million (£2.15 million).

Kim Clijsters plays Venus Williams at the 2009 US Open. Clijsters won the tournament in 2009 and 2010.

The Davis Cup

In 1900, a US team of Harvard University students played and defeated a tennis team from Great Britain. It was the first International Lawn Tennis Challenge, which became the Davis Cup, the biggest annual men's team tennis competition in the world.

FINDOM
BNP PARIB

Getting into groups

Around 130 nations enter the Davis Cup. Teams are placed in three regional zones (Americas, Europe/Africa and Asia/Oceania). Above these zones is the 16-team World Group. Every year, the bottom eight World Group teams play-off against the top teams from the zones. The winners of those ties play in the World Group the following year.

Rubbers and ties

Teams are drawn to play each other in a tie, which is a series of five tennis matches. Each match is known as a rubber. Two singles matches are played, then a doubles match and finally, two more singles matches.

Tomáš Berdych of the Czech Republic serves in the final of the 2013 Davis Cup. The Czech Republic beat Serbia 3-0 to lift the Davis Cup.

The World Group competition

The top 16 teams take part in the World Group competition each season. Only teams in this group can harbour dreams of winning that year's Davis Cup. The 16 teams play a four-round knockout competition, with the rounds spaced out during the year. The final tie is usually played at the end of the tennis season in late November or early December.

In a 2009 Davis Cup semi-final rubber, Croatia's Ivo Karlović hit an incredible 78 aces. Yet, he still lost the match to the Czech Republic's Radek Štěpánek, 7-6, 6-7, 6-7, 7-6, 14-16.

Memorable moments

In 1996, the final between France and Sweden went to the fifth and last set of the fifth rubber, with France eventually beating Sweden. Four years later, Spain became the tenth different country to win the Davis Cup when they defeated Australia 3-1. In 2004, an 18-year-old Rafael Nadal helped Spain to another victory, and they won again in 2008, 2009 and 2011, but the USA has garnered the most wins overall, with 32 Davis Cup victories.

The US Davis Cup team celebrate after beating Russia to win the 2007 trophy.

The Federation Cup

The Federation Cup (Fed Cup) is the women's equivalent of the Davis Cup. It was first held in 1963 and takes place every year. Four countries – Australia, Great Britain, France and Italy – have competed in every single year of the competition.

Fed Cup format

National teams are placed in groups. The top group is the eight-team World Group, and below that a further eight teams are placed in World Group II. The World Group teams play up to three ties – in effect, a quarter-final, semi-final and a final. Each tie comprises five matches – four singles and finally, a doubles match. A team needs to win three matches to secure victory in the tie and progress to the next round.

Ai Sugiyama, of Japan, returns the ball to Ana Ivanovic of Serbia during a Fed Cup World Group II tie in Belgrade, Serbia.

Italy beat the USA 3–1 in the 2010 Fed Cup final, held in San Diego, USA.

Rise and fall

Losing the first round game in the Fed Cup World Group I puts a team under enormous pressure. They then play a tie against a World Group II team, and if they also lose that they will be relegated into World Group II. Spain, for example, won their first Fed Cup in 1991 and have won four more since then, but two losses in 2009 saw them start the 2010 competition in World Group II. In 2015, they narrowly avoided a relegation to the regional groups.

Winning teams

Traditionally, the USA has been the strongest Fed Cup team. It has won the competition 17 times in total, but has not secured a victory since 2000. Recent winners have all come from Europe, including Italy, the 2006, 2009, 2010 and 2013 champions.

Tennis at the Olympics

Tennis was one of nine sports at the very first modern Olympics, held in Athens in 1896. It remained in the Olympics until 1924, when contention about **amateurs** and professionals saw it dropped as an Olympic sport until 1988. Some have questioned whether it should be part of the Olympics, but recent tournaments have been both surprising and inspiring.

Getting to the Games

There are four tennis competitions at the Olympics – men's and women's singles and doubles, but since 2012, mixed doubles have also been included. Most players qualify based on their tour ranking position. A small number are given wild card invitations to take part.

Team GB's Andy Murray claims Olympic gold in the men's singles at the 2012 Olympics.

Medal winners

Winning an Olympic title sees a player awarded ranking points, but what players are after is one of sport's most prestigious prizes, an Olympic medal. These can mean more to players than any cash prize. First, second and third places receive gold, silver and bronze medals. In 1988 and 1992, the two losing semi-finalists each received a bronze medal, but since 1996 they have had to play a further match for a single bronze medal.

Surprises and shocks

In the 1992 Olympics, the world's top five players, including Germany's Boris Becker and the USA's Pete Sampras, took part in the competition, but it was Switzerland's Marc Rosset who won the gold. Another shock occurred in 2004 when Nicolás Massú from Chile took gold in both the singles and the men's doubles.

The 2012 Olympics

The London Olympics in 2012 saw Andy Murray defeat Roger Federer to take gold in the men's singles. Murray became the first British man to win the Olympic singles gold medal since 1908. In the women's singles, Serena Williams defeated Maria Sharapova in the final, losing just one game. She also defended the women's doubles title with her sister, Venus. The Williams sisters became the first four-time gold medallists in Olympic tennis history, having also won the women's doubles in 2000 and 2008.

GREAT SPORTING STATS

Kathleen McKane Godfree holds the record for the most Olympic tennis medals, with one gold, two silvers and two bronzes. Unluckiest has been Spanish player Arantxa Sánchez Vicario, winning two bronzes and two silvers, but never gold.

At the 2008 Olympics, all three medals in the women's singles were won by Russian players – Dinara Safina (left), Elena Dementieva (centre) and Vera Zvonareva (right).

1877 First Wimbledon Championships for men only.

1881 First US Open (called the US National Men's Singles Championship) is held in Newport, Rhode Island.

1884 First women at Wimbledon Championships.

1891 First French Open.

1900 Davis Cup starts.

1905 First Australian Open Championships held.

1922 Seeding used for the first time, at the United States National Championships.

1925 French Open allows non-French players to take part for the first time.

1926 First professional tennis tour begins, featuring famous players of the era playing exhibition matches.

1950 Australia begins domination of the Davis Cup, winning the competition 15 times in 18 years.

1963 Federation Cup founded.

1969 Australian Rod Laver wins his second calendar Grand Slam (all four Grand Slam tournaments in a year), the last to occur in men's singles tennis.

1971 Tie-break system employed at Wimbledon for the first time.

1973 Women's Tennis Association (WTA) formed.

1978 Martin Navratilova wins the first of her 18 career Grand Slam tournaments.

1978 US Open moves from Forest Hills to Flushing Meadows, New York City.

1984 US players Martina Navratilova and Pam Shriver begin an epic run of eight Grand Slam women's doubles titles in a row (1984–85).

1988 Tennis returns as an Olympic sport.

1988 Steffi Graf achieves a Golden Slam, winning all four Grand Slam events and an Olympic gold medal.

1990 ATP Tour begins.

2006 Hawk-Eye instant replay system for line calls is used at its first Grand Slam tournament, the US Open.

2012 Roger Federer wins his seventh Wimbledon title (his 17th Grand Slam title) at the age of 30.

2012 Sisters Serena and Venus Williams become the first four-time Olympic gold medallists in tennis history.

American player Don Budge plays a backhand shot during the 1938 Wimbledon tournament. Budge won a total of six grand slam tournaments.

Winner tables

Australian Open Champions

Year	Men	Women
2015	Novak Djokovic (Serbia)	Serena Williams (USA)
2014	Stanislas Wawrinka (Switzerland)	Li Na (China)
2013	Novak Djokovic (Serbia)	Victoria Azarenka (Belarus)
2012	Novak Djokovic (Serbia)	Victoria Azarenka (Belarus)
2011	Novak Djokovic (Serbia)	Kim Clijsters (Belgium)
2010	Roger Federer (Switzerland)	Serena Williams (USA)
2009	Rafael Nadal (Spain)	Serena Williams (USA)
2008	Novak Djokovic (Serbia)	Maria Sharapova (Russia)
2007	Roger Federer (Switzerland)	Serena Williams (USA)
2006	Roger Federer (Switzerland)	Amélie Mauresmo (France)
2005	Marat Safin (Russia)	Serena Williams (USA)

French Open Champions

Year	Men	Women
2015	Stanislas Wawrinka (Switzerland)	Serena Williams (USA)
2014	Rafael Nadal (Spain)	Maria Sharapova (Russia)
2013	Rafael Nadal (Spain)	Serena Williams (USA)
2012	Rafael Nadal (Spain)	Maria Sharapova (Russia)
2011	Rafael Nadal (Spain)	Li Na (China)
2010	Rafael Nadal (Spain)	Francesca Schiavone (Italy)
2009	Roger Federer (Switzerland)	Svetlana Kuznetsova (Russia)
2008	Rafael Nadal (Spain)	Ana Ivanović (Serbia)
2007	Rafael Nadal (Spain)	Justine Henin (Belgium)
2006	Rafael Nadal (Spain)	Justine Henin (Belgium)
2005	Rafael Nadal (Spain)	Justine Henin (Belgium)

Wimbledon Champions

Year	Men	Women
2015	Novak Djokovic (Serbia)	Serena Williams (USA)
2014	Novak Djokovic (Serbia)	Petra Kvitová (Czech Republic)
2013	Andy Murray (UK)	Marian Bartoli (France)
2012	Roger Federer (Switzerland)	Serena Williams (USA)
2011	Novak Djokovic (Serbia)	Petra Kvitová (Czech Republic)
2010	Rafael Nadal (Spain)	Serena Williams (USA)
2009	Roger Federer (Switzerland)	Serena Williams (USA)
2008	Rafael Nadal (Spain)	Venus Williams (USA)
2007	Roger Federer (Switzerland)	Venus Williams (USA)
2006	Roger Federer (Switzerland)	Amélie Mauresmo (France)
2005	Roger Federer (Switzerland)	Venus Williams (USA)

US Open Champions

Year	Men	Women
2015	Novak Djokovic (Serbia)	Flavia Pennetta (Italy)
2014	Marin Čilić (Croatia)	Serena Williams (USA)
2013	Rafael Nadal (Spain)	Serena Williams (USA)
2012	Andy Murray (UK)	Serena Williams (USA)
2011	Novak Djokovic (Serbia)	Samantha Stosur (Australia)
2010	Rafael Nadal (Spain)	Kim Clijsters (Belgium)
2009	Juan Martín del Potro (Argentina)	Kim Clijsters (Belgium)
2008	Roger Federer (Switzerland)	Serena Williams (USA)
2007	Roger Federer (Switzerland)	Justine Henin (Belgium)
2006	Roger Federer (Switzerland)	Maria Sharapova (Russia)
2005	Roger Federer (Switzerland)	Kim Clijsters (Belgium)

Glossary and further info

Ace A serve that the opposing player is unable to get their racquet to and return.

Advantage When one player wins the first point from a deuce and needs one more point to win the game.

Amateurs Players who are not paid to take part in tennis tournaments.

ATP The Association of Tennis Professionals. The organisation that runs men's professional tennis.

Clay court season A period of the year (usually April to June or July) when most top professional tournaments are played on clay courts.

Deuce The score 40–40 in a game. A player must win two consecutive points from a deuce before winning the game.

Elite The top professional tennis players.

Grand Slam The nickname of the four biggest tournaments of the year – the Australian, French and US Opens plus Wimbledon. It also means to win all four of these tournaments in a single year.

Knockout A tennis competition format in which winning players advance to the next round while those who lose are eliminated from the contest.

Mixed doubles A tennis competition in which each team has one male and one female player.

Professional Tennis players who make their living by competing in tournaments.

Round robin A tournament format where all the competitors in a group play each other.

Seeded The top players in a tournament. The matches are drawn in a way that prevents seeded players from playing each other in the earliest rounds of a competition.

Semi-final Two tennis matches played before the final. The winners of the semi-final matches face off in the finals.

Serve The powerful overhead shot that is used to start each point in tennis.

Serve and volley A tennis tactic where the server moves in towards the net straight after serving. The server looks to win the point by making a volley.

Stadia The plural of stadium, large venues where major tournament matches may be played.

Tie-break The system used in many competitions to end a set after the scores are tied at six games each.

Veterans Tennis players who have been active in the sport for a long time.

Volley Hitting a return shot before the ball can bounce.

WTA The Women's Tennis Association. The organisation that runs women's professional tennis.

Websites

http://www.ausopen.com
The official website of the Australian Open contains a detailed event guide with historical features, as well as news of recent tournaments.

http://www.rolandgarros.com/index.html
The official website of Roland Garros which holds the French Open every year.

http://www.wimbledon.com
Wimbledon's website has a wealth of information about the tournament, its great matches and its champions.

http://www.usopen.org
The official website of the US Open competition carries a wealth of photos, videos and features about the most recent tournament, and champions lists as well as details of earlier matches.

http://www.daviscup.com
The official website of the Davis Cup contains a complete playing guide showing the breakdowns of the different groups and matches.

http://www.fedcup.com
The Fed Cup website includes an explanation of how countries are ranked, as well as news of all the ties played around the world.

http://www.itftennis.com/olympics
Read about tennis at the Olympics at these International Tennis Federation webpages.

http://www.atpworldtour.com
The Association of Tennis Professionals (ATP) website is full of features, biographies and results records of leading players.

http://www.wtatour.com
The official website for the Women's professional tennis tour, the WTA. Here, you can see in-depth news, competitions and player profiles.

http://www.lta.org.uk
This is the homepage of the Lawn Tennis Association, the organisation that runs tennis in the UK.

http://www.ontennis.com
A good general site for tennis containing the basic rules of the game as well as tournament views and opinions.

Further reading

EDGE Dream to Win: Andy Murray – Roy Apps (Franklin Watts, 2012)
Discover Andy Murray's inspirational life story in this illustrated biography

Know Your Sport: Tennis – Clive Gifford (Franklin Watts, 2012)
Find out about tennis tactics and techniques and read profiles of some of the world's biggest players.

Tennis: Know The Game – Lawn Tennis Association (A&C Black Ltd, 2010)
A comprehensive introduction to tennis. Learn about the rules of the game, the equipment used and the skills needed to succeed.

Index